TAP DANCING ON THE RAZOR'S EDGE

For the Love of Words!

TAP DANCING ON THE RAZOR'S EDGE

Paul A. Lubenkov

Poems by Paul A. Lubenkov

David Robert Books

2018

© 2018 by Paul A. Lubenkov

Published by David Robert Books

P.O. Box 541106

Cincinnati, OH 45254-1106

ISBN: 9781625492722

Poetry Editor: Kevin Walzer

Business Editor: Lori Jareo

Cover design: Margaret Prescott, www.PrescottArtStudio.com

Visit us on the web at www.davidrobertbooks.com

Acknowledgments

The author thanks the editors of the following publications where some of the poems in this volume have appeared or have been scheduled for publication.

Burningword Literary Journal: "Observations In Lieu Of An Elegy," "The Miracle"

The Carolina Quarterly: "Places We Must Go," "When She Would Come"

The Coe Review: "Home Of The Brave," "When Financial Meltdown Strikes Again, What Will Jamie Dimon Do?"

Contemporary American Voices: "The Sower," "What The Horoscope Said," "Les Fauves: Radical Invention," "Ghost Town," "What My Grandma Said"

Fresh Ink: "Vision"

The Outrider Review: "Late Apology"

Panoplyzine: "An Invitation"

River Poets Journal: "In Lieu Of Love"

Smeuse: "Milo De Milo's Seaside Lullaby"

Snapdragon: A Journal Of Art & Healing: "To A Good Friend's Youngest Son Who Committed Suicide"

Soundings East: "The Red-Headed Stepchild Has Words For His Father"

The Sierra Nevada Review: "Elegy For A Japanese Mother"

The Stillwater Review: "No Fool"

The Tule Review: "In Red Wing, Minnesota," "Seven Thoughts For My Father

Where the Mind Dwells: Contemplation: "Variations On Mystic Wisdom

*It's very subtle The Continental
Because it does what you want it to do.*
　　　　　　　　—Fred Astaire

Irony of ironies, all is irony.
　　　　　　　—Thomas Mann

I have said what I had to say.
　　　　　　　—John Berryman

For Terry Anne

her relentless patience and support

Table of Contents

I. Early Awakenings

Ghost Town..19

The Sower...20

Second Thoughts...21

Places We Must Go..22

Inscape...24

When She Would Come...25

Beau Geste Au Naturel...26

What The Horoscope Said..27

The Miracle...28

The Red-Headed Stepchild Has Words For His Father....29

The Journey..30

Home Of The Brave...31

Observations In Lieu Of An Elegy................................32

Discovered In The Shithouse..34

The Male Chauvinist's Rebuttal....................................35

What My Grandma Said 36

II. The Milo De Milo Cycle

Let's Hit The Road: Milo De Milo's Love Song...................................39

Milo De Milo as Dance Critic..40

Milo De Milo's Request for Renewal...41

Milo De Milo Meets His Match..42

Milo De Milo's Litmus Test..43

Milo De Milo, In Delirium, Absorbs The Big Bang Theory.............44

Good Advice From Milo De Milo..45

Milo De Milo's Late Apology...46

Milo De Milo Transcendent...47

Milo De Milo's Fantasy 48

Milo De Milo's Late Night Lament..49

O To Be Milo De Milo: The Gift..50

When Milo De Milo Quotes J. Wellington Wimpy...........................51

Milo De Milo's Advice To Daughters..52

The Enigma Of Milo De Milo...53

Milo De Milo's Seaside Lullaby 54

III. Amuse Bouche

Vision..59

Riposte..60

Confession..61

Regrets..62

The Rub..63

Kalamazoo..64

Small Change..65

Contemplation..66

Temptation...67

IV. The End of the Line

My Gift..71

Balance...72

No Fool...73

Seven Thoughts For My Father...74

Les Fauves: Radical Invention..75

When Financial Meltdown Strikes Again 76

Elegy For A Japanese Mother..77

Variations On Mystic Wisdom..79

Meet Me There...80

Dusk In Huangshan, China 82

To A Good Friend's Youngest Son Who Committed Suicide.........83

Just Saying..84

In Red Wing, Minnesota..86

In Lieu of Love...87

The Love Song Of Leopold And Loeb..............................88

Girl Remembered...92

Pharaoh Of The Stolen Name...93

Last Request...95

An Invitation..96

The End Of The Line...97

Patterns...98

श्र श्र श्र

I.   Early Awakenings

Ghost Town

In deserted houses, floorboards speak
For the strangest reasons. When shutters bang
Or an unwatched door suddenly swings shut,
We say it is the wind when there is
No wind. Birds, rats, shifting foundations.
We are quick with answers that keep the peace,
But who can be sure? On every wall
Moonlight illuminates subtle designs
And these patches of light survive us to say
The past does not die. We let it escape.

The Sower

*Oh! those who don't believe in
this sun here are real infidels.*
      —Vincent Van Gogh

There is no brighter sky. Deep
And wide, these colors reach
Beyond themselves, each short
Stroke of speed assaulted
By light until it must burst
And the trembling land glow
Beneath this magnificent sun.
What more could there be? What man
Could resist the power here, the air
Of imminent explosion? And yet,
Toiling in the right foreground,
This wooden-shoed peasant,
His head too large, his arms
Too short, and on his face
A look of angry desperation,
Does not sow this ground
With the proper reverence.
Scattering an apronful
Of seed in an act of what
Appears to be spastic
Convulsion, he strides toward
Something out of sight.
His hat low on his neck, he is leaving
Behind him that sun, that sky,
The half-sowed fields as if
He imagined he could somehow
Abandon them, escape to some
Other place where he could teach
His shadow to believe in something
Anything except this impossible sun.

Second Thoughts

It is always too late. When you reach
The brink and your left foot drags the right
Right over the edge, when everything
Backs up far away, leaving no tracks,
It happens. It all falls into place.
Jubilant cries of cavalry split
The air, the marines land, that sulky
Saint Bernard lumbers himself up and
Over the last frozen hill and, yes,
My friend, there is no mistaking it now,
The time has come. The moment you spread
Yourself on the wind, just as you kiss
The fatal air good-bye, indulging,
Perhaps, in your favorite gestures of
Defiance and disgust, when the whole
Preposterous affair seems right, then
The truth arrives, slightly late and
Breathless, to tell you its secret at last.

Places We Must Go

Every day this monstrous blot of
Mustard on the far horizon must
Shrivel up and flake away.

When all that's left are just
Some distant stains of light,
Your eyes may take you where

Dark shapes are pushing past you
On the empty plains and far away.
That will be us you see. And if

Your ear is good and he is not
Somewhere deep in dreams of fire,
Then you may hear my father sing

Of women I have never known. Softly
Always. His voice the moonlight which
Makes floors of old homes speak.

No longer does my father know
Who I am, or even that I
Push him places we must go,

Trailing sparks of light behind
The wheels of his silver chair. But,
Because he once was fond of trees,

We stop to watch them lift their limbs
Pointing at things between the stars.
Then his eyes tighten on memories

And he sings of ladies thin and starched,
How the meat is sweeter closer to the bone.
His voice slips into the night, grinds

Softly against the spinning dark,
Hot slivers slicing away.
When he is still, we listen for

The dark water that slowly gathers
In the distance. He told me once
That at the heart of every fire, is fire.

Inscape

But internal differences
Where the meanings are
—Emily Dickinson

These times are no times
For strong men. Each day
Yesterday arrives
Too soon. I hear it
Disguised as the wind
And sniffing for blood,
Perhaps mine. Then sunlight
Warps the room as I
Fall from my bed into
Myself, amazed at
What is waiting there.
Outside, the world may
Rant and rave in the
Outrageous fashion
Of the day. Let it.
I shall struggle through
Life with a tight ass
Hole on my own dark
Universe and say it's
Weird enough for me.

When She Would Come

On the coldest of nights whenever sickness came
She made us well. Our teeth she counted backward
As her eyes began to dance. And there were songs,
Words we did not understand, smells
We could not recognize, and soup we did not want:
Huge bowls of steaming blood heavy with herbs
And sacs of grease so thick on top that red
Clouds would catch the light above and glow.
She held our eyes with hers and made us drink,
And warm with that potent soup we fought off sleep,
Then watched her drink down all that we left
Wiping off like a smile those sticky drops
Dangling from mustached lips. And as her face,
Damp with sweat and dim in the shifting dark
Slowly began to wax with light and glow,
Our dreams would begin to glow, and in those dreams
That light of hers would follow as she moved
Through empty rooms where nothing ever changed,
And with every move she made her bones would sing.

Beau Geste Au Naturel

Gutless in Gaza is no
Way to be but I am. The deep
Hunger for stone is a joke
Out here, and where is that voice
Hung with slow thunder
Ready to save the day?
Ringing their wild bells and
Dressed to kill, the shrewd
Natives come dragging slabs
Of salt across the sun.
They know nothing succeeds
Like success, that no price is too great
For pain. When the birds begin
To descend, only a fool
Confounded by dreams and things
Like honour tries to resist
The last bribe and breath of sun.
We learn to create our needs,
Not die for them. If iron
Remembered the blood it lived,
Things might be different. But that
Is not so. The Dead Sea is
No metaphor, and all those
Beautiful gestures turn out
The same when all is said and
Done because peristalsis,
That last involuntary
Shrug, just about says it all.

What The Horoscope Said

For George Garrett

Maintain your balance: avoid the new,
Forget the old. When the telephone rings,
Study the hollow sound of air.
Waving the loud flag of love,

A mysterious woman shall enter your life.
It will be too late. Remember the mailman,
And spend some time resisting pain.
The silence of wisdom is everywhere;

Bite your tongue and listen for fools.
Enjoy whatever pleasures you can,
But avoid the night, all those trees
Shaking their arms of dark thunder.

With luck, you will keep one jump ahead
Of whatever is always somewhere behind,
So forget that hand, that web of bone
Scratching its way across your wall.

The sun will set and nothing will happen.
The moon will rise and nothing will change.
A blind man will bring you a terrible gift,
And you will remember what you tried to forget.

The Miracle

Who could ever imagine this breach
Of sun? Not even the priests
Grazed by the moon and eager
To serve could say for sure. Oh,
They fasted, wept, and prayed. With
The passion of despair, they
Brought hundreds to the knife. Lord,
The stench. Baskets stuffed with soft
Steaming entrails. But nowhere
Was an answer to be found.
Encouraged, then, by what they
Could not see, they counted up
Their blessings in disguise. They
Danced, they sang, they fell back on
Tradition and, praising all
Such miracles of mystery,
They blessed the bloody fields.

The Red-Headed Stepchild Has Words For His Father

Failure is fun and teaches us our names.
Father, you were ripe with wit. I remember your mouth
Gorged with tongue, how your eyes were stung with rust.
You spoke to your fist and shook it in my face.

Dreams, you would say. *I hold dreams waiting for freedom.*
I tried to imagine your words rising like birds
Beating against the wind. Then you opened that fist
And your hand swept through the sky like a white flame.

Each day you drank yourself closer to death, and I watched
Waiting for a good word. But I waited for nothing.
You taught me that words were empty threats from the dead,
And your rage brought up blood each time I called you *Father.*

One night you slapped me awake and told me, *Dying*
Is a fact of life. But take it with a grain of salt.
I did, old man, I took you at your word,
And why not? The dead have no claims on the living.

The prayers I promised you rattle like phlegm in my throat.
A stranger to my own blood, I will live out your lies
Forgetting forever the sounds we dragged through dreams,
Cries of vultures beating their wings with love.

The Journey

The footprints behind me are not
mine not the footprints I dragged
far from the distance of dark seas
darker skies a place where
whatever is lost is home not
following now not in this place
this country with flags describing the sun
a sun like nothing I can remember
not like this in another sky
a different wind with its own banners
and stars falling from black fields
stars that could almost be lost friends
falling with silence but not this silence
always arriving with nowhere to go.

Home Of The Brave

Just look at these freaks they're nowhere and everywhere half
in love with their great hunger and stuffing themselves with
succulent meals of soft white food but what do they care they
don't care about towers of silence the great perishing trees how
even on the clearest days something is always blurring the sky
why they don't know grunt from gravy these freaks these weirdos
and even though once and with rubber gloves I approached their warm
temple of sleep to amaze them by crying, *Lo! Practitioners of Peace,
Arise!* but I was nothing to them if not something escaped from
The Ed Sullivan Show raving around with my own banner these slick
scars on review which they were unable to see so well or appreciate
pain betrayed as they are by an obvious absence of clear direction
within their eyes the blue spilling out into rivers seas skies whatever
remains to accept it and so cannot see what the moon is about its
gross flatulence smearing across the recently featureless land in thick
layers like mayonnaise over which and in disgust the last butterfly
screams its final scream and barbarous tongues grow teeth to say
the clarion calls to violence rise are rising have risen at last. Listen:

Observations In Lieu Of An Elegy

Scooter Monzingo is dead.
The weather is crisp, the streets
Are exceptionally clean.
His wife is amazed at how
Natural he looks, the way
His fingers gracefully mesh.

It is six o'clock. In Rome,
In a cheap villa, a young
American housewife is
Seducing a gigolo.
She insists his name is Frank.
What an ugly word! Franck thinks.

It is six o'clock. Demure
Millie Hobbes is pawning her
Gramophone. She has plans, big
Plans. Someday her neighbors will
See her and say, *Who would have
Thought it?* She can hardly wait.

It is six o'clock. Rainstorms
Lash the coast of Uruguay.
In a crowded marketplace,
A slow-eyed senorita
Has begun to menstruate
For the first time. People stare.

If he were alive today,
Scooter Monzingo would say
4,800 words,
Move 700 muscles,
Eat over 3 pounds of food,
And breathe. Which is average.

Discovered In The Shithouse

Written on the wall that each man reads,
Etched deeper than the darkest dreams
With those bodies like erector sets
Trapped forever in their awkward act,
Needing no number, verb, or rhyme,
No artist's sketch or clever phrase,
My name sprawls across the wall,
Immortalized in this shithouse stall.

Some men might laugh, wondering why,
Or consider adding a word of wit,
But you learn to live with things like that.
It's like The Phantom Shitter wrote:
The price of fame is always high,
But life is more than reason's peanut.

The Male Chauvinist's Rebuttal

You beast! she cried and charged out
The door throwing not spears but
Weird allusions to missing
Keys, cages, caves, and the late
Great American asshole.
Well, what did she expect?
Those love poems she called hors d'oeuvres
Just weren't enough. It's like
The old prospector said. You
Give a man a meal and he eats,
But only a fool marries
His meal. And it works both ways.
When her teeth were hooves gashing
Their tracks in my flesh did I
Ever complain about her
Primitive tendencies? No,
A man must remain a man.
So what if *Buffalo Bill*
Is defunct. His legacy lives,
And I could care less about
The great buffalo slaughters.
Those homogenized misfits
Tucked safely away in zoos
Seem not to be legends but
Discarded trophies whose stunned
Eyes keep asking, *What am I
Doing here?* She got the point.

What My Grandma Said

From a Czech proverb

No matter how sad
Do not trust the man
Who never wants to sing.

He will bore you to death
With the speech of the deaf
And your ears will turn to stone.

II. *The Milo De Milo Cycle*

Let's Hit The Road:
Milo De Milo's Love Song

You told me, "I know
  You do not know
What you do not know
  Or possibly care,
So why then should I!"
  Well in my defense
I answered: What
  About me if not
About you these swans
  Glazing silver
Ponds unbroken
  Chrysanthemums
Their slow perfection
  Out of reach
Empty temples
  Open doors.
Or imagine this,
  Just you and me
Cruising the country
  Soft top down
Pollen in hair
  The world at our feet.
I mean what I mean
  And we are who we are
'Cause the nut's in its shell.
  So believe me if
It's just this once
  When once is enough.
Come on, it's time.
  Just give me a try!

Milo De Milo as Dance Critic

I never saw an odalisque
 Perform a raunchy arabesque,
But I lust and sweat and turn to jell-o
 When my lady does the saltarello.

Milo De Milo's Request for Renewal

When the light comes back
 From wherever it's been,
Will you clap your hands and
 Make love begin again?

Milo De Milo Meets His Match

I figured you knew
The *Spanish Flye*
Was no dance
In the classical style.
But when you said,
"I know a fool
When I see one,
And I can see
Through you. *Let's Dance!*"
I knew you were
Just right for me.

Milo De Milo's Litmus Test

And so you sing a song to me
  And I sing one back at you,
Then I fantasize what night might bring
  When our raunchy words turn blue.

Milo De Milo, In Delirium, Absorbs The Big Bang Theory

  I wasn't ever here before
  But then, like *that* , I came
And the world that split that I might be
  Was never quite the same.

Good Advice From Milo De Milo

You should never say never to more
Or people will think you're a bore.
And never imagine that it might be a mess.
There lies incredible beauty in life lived to excess.

Milo De Milo's Late Apology

And so what else
Was I to do,
Lovely girl,
So long ago?
You, so thin
Of bone, so pearl
Of skin, you danced
Like a dream in your black
Cocktail dress
While I drank until
I could no more.
Then the ride back home
With the heaving whirlies
As irresistible
As your perfect eyes,
Your long milk legs,
Those crème fraiche thighs.
And so what else
Was I to do
But retch, then hurl
Up all over you?
So, so sorry.

Milo De Milo Transcendent

Try to imagine what dawn might bring
  When eros flips to agape and two
Hearts raise celestial voice and sing,
  Love is more than just some goo.

Milo De Milo's Fantasy

Fifi,
      DeeDee,
Mimi,
      CeeCee,
Gigi,
      BeeBee,
 Titi,
      Oui Oui.
Olé !

Milo De Milo's Late Night Lament

So you sit there in the dark alone
 Wondering what might have been,
Who you might have taken home
 But not this pillow reeking gin.

O To Be Milo De Milo: The Gift

Milo is lit and living life large.
Enough of this boxing away with flies
Incessantly fracking around the skull.
Dressed to the nines and greased to the gills,
He knows he could make any chicky moan
Like a well-oiled alto saxophone.
He is out and about for the stiff one,
Ready to put the kibosh on anyone
Blocking his way. See the dude
Tap dancing on the razor's edge,
Taking the old bull by the balls,
A King Farouk looking for love.
He is one spicy meatball, ripped
And ready to rumble. So I sent him to you.

When Milo De Milo Quotes J. Wellington Wimpy

"I will gladly pay you Tuesday
 "For a hamburger today,"
That's the style of hungry finance
All the Big Banks love to play.

Milo De Milo's Advice To Daughters

The good witch said, "Don't pick the man
    Who never wants to sing.
The moon won't shine, the seas won't sigh,
    And your bell will never ring.

The Enigma Of Milo De Milo

If Milo De Milo
Were not Milo De Milo
And never could possibly be;
Then consider the possibilities:
How maybe he could be you
Or perhaps he might really be me.

Milo De Milo's Seaside Lullaby

Milo stands
At the start of the sea

Or the end of the sea or
Perhaps at the edge

Of the sea. Who knows
For sure. The thing is

The man is at peace.
These sea grapes shrugging

Their way to shore
The rhythm of the waves

They leave him content and
He doesn't know why.

All this means something
And Milo knows this but

Perhaps nothing more.
He is sorting it out.

He is giving it shape
And getting it straight

Or not. Sometimes
Things just fall

Into place. They click.
Consider the sound of

A Zoot Sims solo,
The perfection of jazz

As his lonely saxophone
Romances the night.

So the deal is this:
The important thing

Is that Milo stands
Somewhere by the sea and

The man is at peace.
And he hasn't a clue.

III. ***Amuse Bouche***

Vision

You can see
Anger in the eye.
A red horse riding
Across the sun.

Riposte

You insist I revere
The desire in your heart,
The fire in your skull.
Then my blood darks.

Confession

In this mystery of heat,
We briefly fuse together,

More love than I deserve,
More flesh than I remember.

Regrets

But life
Always seems
To get in the way.

The Rub

Every one of us stands
In the last place we were,
So enjoy whatever you can.
But does anyone know
If any will be
In some other next place again?

Kalamazoo

How some words
　　Do sing
　To themselves.

Small Change

The future is not
What it used to be.
Neither is the present.

Contemplation

How
Will the darkness
Fall?

Temptation

And who can neglect
The irresolute pain
Of the locked door?

The whorled grain
And burnished doorknob
Are irresistible.

IV. The End of the Line

My Gift

I have no house
Only a shadow,
But whenever you
Are in need of a shadow,
My shadow is yours.

Balance

To feel a loss a certain
Dizzy loss in the sense
The sense of *equilibrium*
Is natural my GP says,
Part of the aging process.
Equilibrium, yes,
Which sounds so much better than just
Getting old, which is when
And where the mind plays tricks,
As how the exotic names
Of these faded glamour girls
Shimmering back in my childhood
Randomly come to mind,
Ida Lupino, Zsa Zsa
Gabor, Gina Lollobrigida,
Impenetrable memories
Cooing in the gentle wind
From a vague and distant landscape,
Leading inexorably away
From where I want to be,
Away from where I need
To be, feet on the ground,
Solid, and not this distinct
Loss of balance, spinning
Away, unhinged, unglued,
Not equilibrium but *balance,*
With a disturbing loss of balance,
With the sense of what that means,
And with, oh yes, Brigitte Bardot.

No Fool

The cynic said,
"When you fall in love
And throw down your heart
For some sweet thing,

Know that someone, somewhere
Has grown weary of her,
So suspend yourself
Between her lies."

And my beauty explained
How a good old fool
Was so hard to find,
But now she had me.

Then she glowed in the night
With the wit of the moon,
While each of her smiles
Swept my heart clean.

Seven Thoughts For My Father

After the funeral
We learn to suffer.

Old men with umbrellas
Lean into the wind.

You are layers of air,
The twist of water.

I remember your color,
Stones in the night.

Your face had to say
What your words could not say.

Now, day after day
The dry wind blows,

And the wind that remains
Is the shape of your pain.

Les Fauves: Radical Invention

*It has bothered me all my life that
I don't paint like everyone else.
— Henri Matisse*

But, the color ! Your brilliant color!

Slabs of aromatic blue,
Stripes of iridescent green,
Goldfish struck like stamped medallions
Suspended in a bowl of ether.

You opened windows to bold cathedrals,
Moroccan landscapes redolent with spice,
Aberrant hues and the falling light
That bleaches color and flattens form.

Your loving and confident hands caressed
Breath to canvas. Languorous nudes
Embrace their moment as eyebrows evolve
Curving to aquiline nose, just so.

Carving with color, your brushstrokes stung,
Left Salon dandies dazed and dumb,
Eyeballs scorched by the glorious light.

That mystic beard you wore with such grace
Did not muffle your growls for perfection.
And what dull brute could tame this delicate beast?

When Financial Meltdown Strikes Again, What Will Jamie Dimon Do?

> *I'll come and foreclose, get your car and your clothes,*
> *Singin' I'm jolly banker, jolly banker am I.*
> — Woody Guthrie

The odds are long, the threat is huge,
And dark clouds litter the horizon
While yesterday's red meat turns bad.
The smiling Shell Answer Man
Is nowhere to be found, my friend,
And lonely Mister Clean, singing
 "Shrimp boats is a-comin
 Their sails are in sight
 Shrimp boats is a-comin
 There's dancin' tonight,"
Cannot clean up this oily mess.
Each action has its consequence,
And we must account for all this shit
When financial doom stares us down.
So what would Jamie Dimon do?
You bet your ass: He'd bank on you.

Elegy For A Japanese Mother

I suppose if I had lost the war,
I would have been tried as a war criminal.
                    — General Curtis LeMay

They flew below the clouds in streams,
Hotaru, insects of fire to plague
Conurbations of paper and wood.

A mile above their target, aircrews
Dropped a searing rain of flames:
Incendiary clusters, white

Phosphorous, magnesium bombs and
Napalm – an incandescent sheet
To blanket Tokyo at night.

Ryogoku Bridge, gone.
Hamarikyu Gardens, gone.
Shitamachi District, gone.

Citizens like shards of pottery
Lay scattered on streets and doorsteps.
Aircrews reported that the stench

Of acrid sweat and cremating flesh
Permeated the tailing aircraft,
Lingered in their grotesque dreams.

Did they see you, widow and mother,
Fleeing past Koizumi factory
Through blasts of steam that taste of ash,

Your daughter in your arms? "Aozora," you cried.
"Aozora." But no *blue skies* remain.
Did they see you by the basho tree

Kneeling at the banks of the wide Sumida,
Stealing the shape of that sacred river?
Did they see you say good-bye,

Ease her into the languid water,
The dark that covers like a slumberous shawl,
Your flower flowing to Tokyo Bay?

Variations On Mystic Wisdom

—For Lucien Stryk

Wind is the sound
Of one hand clapping.

And I know the lotus
Is destined to survive

All earthly fire.
But when a tree

Falls in the forest
And no man is there

To hear it fall,
Am I still wrong?

Meet Me There

I would prefer
To be polite
And not point out
What you do not think
When you gaily sing,
"Meet me at the fair.
"Don't tell me
"The lights are shining
"Anyplace but there."
But the fact is
In time those lights
Shining at the fair
Like lights everywhere
Will dim and go dark.
Accept it, and
Consider this: the hiker
Out in Glacier Park
Hanging from the cliff,
Waiting for the bear
To pass on the trail,
Hoping to save himself
And not be mauled,
Surprise, surprise,
Will lose his grip.
That's how it goes.
And anyplace but there
Is where Pauline
Trapped in her perils
Should never really be,
Tied to the tracks,
Hoping against hope
For her savior to come,
Save the damsel,
Ride to the sunset.
Hogwash. The ropes
Hold, the train
Arrives on schedule,

And the cowcatcher
Does a bang-up job.
This is the way
It really works.
The perfect marriage
Snaps, unravels
Slowly away.
When what we want
Are smooth sailings,
Happy endings,
The good life forever,
The sad truth is this:
Everything works
Until it breaks.

Dusk In Huangshan, China

Beyond the steps of the Yellow Mountains
  Mist whispers through twisted pines,
And I shiver as the sad music of the moon
  Erases your name. Please forgive me.

To A Good Friend's Youngest Son Who Committed Suicide

Just what were you thinking when you crossed the tracks,
Stood on the trestle as if on schedule,
A smile suspended between the rails?

Did you remember the drug fueled dance
You put on stage and tried to share,
Knife in hand, with your father's new squeeze?

Could you never imagine your mother,
Tight as an oyster, locked in her room?
You whispered in her ear, *My hell is empty.*

What were you thinking suspended there
Between two rails when the shrieking diesel
With its bright light swirling like the eye of God
And your last scream merged?

                                      And just before
Were you thinking of books unread, the scent
Of a girl walking your way, all the games
You could master and play? Just what were you thinking?

Oh, yeah. You were thinking, *I'll show you!*

Just Saying

Unlike the other guys
Who liked to strut and kick,
I never wanted to be
A Radio City Rockette
Working up a sweat
High kicking in chorus lines.

And on the opposite hand
The Mormon Tabernacle Choir
Sounded to my tin ear
Like a loud moan in the desert,
And I was no Pecos Bill
Strumming a sad guitar.

No, for me it would always be
The Mystic Knights of the Sea.
To be anointed in that lodge
With Amos and Andy and The Kingfish,
Escorting Ruby and Saffire
In Amos's funky cab,

The whole night smeared with funk,
Balling the jack, high
Stepping and dressed to the nines,
Seeking love and redemption
In any form or fashion
In or out of the Cotton Club,

Tap dancing in the dark
Where you hear what you do not see,
Hear the sibilant voice of Lightnin'
Slowly speaking in tongues.
And whatever Lightnin' said,
Was saying, was about to say

Hung in the air like a heartache.
With no time for apologies,
Lightin' *knew* what he knew,
And knowing nothing could change
What he knew, he struck a deadpan
For all of us there to see

Then whispered, "Love flows away,
"And away, as it steals your heart,
"So kiss your redemption goodbye.
"I have said what I had to say,
"And that ain't no pig in a poke.
"You got nothing to lose at last."

In Red Wing, Minnesota

When the Amtrak stops
On this warm summer night,
No one gets off and
No one gets on.

Red Wing is asleep.
Light from the streetlamps
Glides like ice
Down empty streets.

In the shuttered Cape Cod
On Hickory Lane,
The windows and mirrors
Debate what remains.

Even the dogs
Out for the night
Hold their ground,
Perplexed with the moon.

In this quaint, small town
They make the shoes
For working men
Who punch the clock,

Who follow the schedules
And mean what they say
As if what they say
Is how they hold

Things together.
These people know
They have it all,
And it's not enough.

In Lieu Of Love

I never planned to take you for a ride
In the flim-flam caravan of love, but
Here we are again, hunkered down
And buck naked in your luminous boudoir
Where your toy animals bear us silent witness.
So let them stare. I will not rise to guilt,
That aching vice, and you, on your behalf,
May rightfully laugh at all my loopy lust
And looney-tune desires. But I tell you this,
Here in this dense capsule we call now,
The time is right and you are ripe as well.
So whether you take me as I am or how
You wish I were, it's all the same to me.
You will never be more voluptuous while I
Shall be as brave and dashing as you desire,
And together we may tease away the night
And cheat the moon. I will have no regrets.

The Love Song Of Leopold And Loeb

> "With our looks and Darrow's brains,
> "I think we'll get along pretty well."
> — Nathan Leopold

I.

It was the crime of the century.
It was the trial of the century.

But the hot and crowded courtroom
Was a rendezvous for Nathan.

Seated next to him was Loeb,
Elegant, beautiful Loeb
With impeccable social skills,
His smug courtroom smile,
The classic line of his jaw,
The lapels of his tailored suits
Sharp as knives to the eye.

Disciples of Friedrich Nietzsche,
Each boy was an *Ubermensch,*
And they made each other complete.

No god of sky and thunder
Could threaten the tower of their dreams,
Their lust for the perfect crime.

II.

Does it matter who took the wheel,
Drove the Willys-Knight death van,
Or who thrust the chisel over
And over into Bobby Frank's
 Soft and yielding brain,
  Bludgeon the child to death?

Of course they were quickly caught,
Confessed with arrogant pride
To their moment of perfect lust.

Eager to join the mob,
Billy Sunday condemned
The moral miasma he saw.
"Precocious brains, salacious
"Books, infidel minds —
"All these produced this murder."

III.

But pleading the two boys guilty,
Darrow denied free will,
Asked how could these boys, although sane,
Be responsible for these crimes,
For these actions so predetermined?

Decorous during the speech,
The words that saved their lives,
Darrow's brilliant summation
Bringing tears from Judge Caverly
Who sentenced these two smug boys
To life plus 99 years,
The boys then reverted to type:

Led by jailers back to their cells,
"Get us two steaks, thick
"And juicy," Loeb demanded.
And his lover Leopold echoed,
"Yes, and make sure they are smothered
"In onions. And bring every side dish."

Two boys moving on with their lives.

IV.

A Chicago Tribune reporter
Stunned by the courtroom's silence
Spoke of history's darker days:

When the cabal that murdered Lincoln
Received judgment and their bodies hung,
They were buried in graves just feet
From the gallows. Then Secretary of War
Stanton cried out, "We wish
"To hear their names no more."

Enough, they cry, is enough.

As they passed through the night to their cells
And their shadows dissolved in the dark,
Who was there to teach these boys,
To imagine the days to pass,
To count the burning stars,
And to kiss the bitter moon good-night?

Enough, as they say, is enough.

Girl Remembered

Some girls you remember
For their oily scent
For the curve of their ass
Or the salt in their sweat.
But you took the stage
With an ode to *soap*.
"People who like people,"
You read, "Like Dial,
"But I prefer Ivory."
And the raking light
Of time did not dull
The bite of your wit.
Was it you or *it*
That still knocks me out?"

Pharaoh Of The Stolen Name

On the night you chose to die,
Your priests threw salt to the heavens,
But it would not rain for days.

They took this as a sign
That you who were a god,
Ruling the children of gods,

Must lose all that you were.
In the deliquescent night,
Royal Wedjat amulets,

Vessels of oil and scarabs,
Your Eye of Horus ring,
Would glow in the hands of thieves.

Hieroglyphs of hammered gold,
Your glory and your name,
Stripped and stolen from your tomb.

So what now do we call you?
Through the false door that opens to heaven,
You pass like a vapor, then sigh.

Trapped between here and now,
You stand naked before your gods,
Not a faience to your name.

Your spirit wanders your tomb
Thin as a whisper in the wind,
Nameless to the keeper of balance.

Each night the dark sky swoons
As your memories dissolve to dreams
Where you write whose name in the sand.

Last Request

If you happen to see me dying,
Be kind. Read me a poem,
Preferably one of mine
With soft edges and dreams.

When my hands start to sweat and shake,
Hold them gently with your hands
As if we were falling in love.

If my tongue starts flapping like a fish
Hooked and thrown to the beach,
Say you hear the music of Mozart.

Then try to imagine my soul
With precious stones and gold
Anxious for the great escape.

At the end, sing me a sweet song
And make *sure* they spell my name right.

An Invitation

After St. John of Nepomuk, Bohemia
Patron Saint of Silence and Flooding

The savant who bit off and swallowed his tongue
Altogether was never a student of history.
The vast Peloponnesian Wars
Meant nothing to him. The Rosetta Stone
Was just a rock, the Dead Sea Scrolls
An oxymoron. But the silence of the night
Washed over him like an indolent sea,
And he knew how the rhythm of flowing water
Was irresistible, why boulders sleep
In dark forests without any fear
While strange animals prowl the streets.
He knows he is here to imagine these things,
To inhale the purple scent of night
As pungent as blood on the tip of the tongue,
And to hold them together in elegant balance.
Listen to the perfect silence of his dreams.

The End Of The Line

As if he were the Oracle of Delphi,
This egg-headed geneticist,
Secure in the mist of academe,
Foretells my inevitable extinction.
This is all about the Y chromosome,
That conglomerate of kinky proteins
Linked to surging nucleotides,
How in time it will decay and mutate
Hurtling down its accelerated
Evolutionary path to oblivion
In a million years.   On the other hand,
A worn-out girlfriend of mine, sly
To the touch, shared this with me: "If
"A cucumber could take out the garbage,
"There would be no need for men." *Poof!*
Extinct. Adding insult to injury,
She pointed out that "size matters." So
It comes down to this, two sides
Of the same coin, my destiny
Displaced by some vegetable *bon mot*.
But what can you do? *Que sera, sera.*
I have no choice but to go with the flow,
And in a million years or so,
Whoever inherits my line will rise
Claiming my birthright, the Lost Son of Onan.

Patterns

Over my morning coffee,
A rich Jamaican blend,
I follow the young cardinal
As he flies from arbor vitae
To blue spruce, from spruce
To arbor vitae, then back again.
Spruce to arbor vitae,
Arbor vitae to spruce.
And this all seems so familiar.

Paul Lubenkov

Paul Lubenkov of La Grange, Illinois has had experience in a wide range of occupations: grinder in an iron foundry, university instructor, benefits analyst, technology sales executive, national account manager, corporate leasing director, and business banking vice president. He currently teaches at Morton College and strongly believes that having multiple careers allows you to live multiple lives.

He is grateful to the following sources of formal education and inspiration:

B.A. in English & Political Science, Cornell College
M.A. in English Literature, Northern Illinois University
Studies with Jim Whitehead, Creative Writing Program, University of Arkansas
M.F.A. in Creative Writing, University of Arizona
B.S. in Business Management, Elmhurst College
Management Certificate Program, Loyola School of Business Administration.

Every stage was a joy and challenge, each in its own way, and I would re-live them all if I could.